SHRINKING INTO INFINITE SKY

Vicki Mandell-King

FUTURECYCLE PRESS

www.futurecycle.org

Library of Congress Control Number: 2015955406

Published by FutureCycle Press
Lexington, Kentucky, USA

ISBN 978-1-938853-84-5

*This book of poems is dedicated to my mother, Roberta,
and to Geraldine (Gerri), my mother-in-law, who was like a second
mother to me. Mother taught me, among other things, sweetness
and forgiveness. Gerri's last four years of life illustrate that death,
by and large, comes on its own terms. Both were great beauties,
full of grace to their very ends—one too soon and unexpected,
the other long-delayed and yearned for.*

CONTENTS

Storytelling   7

I. GRACE

Emptying   11
Give and Take   12
Halfway Home   13
The Manicure   14
Combing Memory   15
The Blue Jar   16
For My Sake   17
A Change in the Weather   18
Shrouded   19
A Change of Mind   20
Getting Down to Basics   22
Snowblind   23

II. LAUGH OR CRY

And What of Humor, Kübler-Ross?   27
Word Choice   28
Taking a Ghost for a Drive   29
Four Breaths   30
A Deathbed Confession   31
Not Really about the Hair   32
You've Got to Be Kidding   33
A Plea for a Witness   34
Dreaming of Oblivion   36
The Die Spot   37

III. TIMING

A Brief Exchange   41
The Time It Takes   42
Not a Suicide   43
Drought's End   44

RSVP   45

Death Wish   46

Box of Divinity   47

We Are All New   48

She Still Surprises Me   49

Dead and I Just Don't Know It   50

Do No Harm   51

IV. AMBIVALENCE

The Ride   55

Just a Few More Steps   56

Touch Is the Last to Go   58

Anticipation   59

Nothing to Do but Wait   60

Welcome and Farewell   61

The Right Question   62

Fate of Tulips   63

Suddenly Aware of Hardening   64

V. QUICKENED

Too Far Gone   67

Undo the Past and Be Done   68

Last Words   69

The Lure of Clay   70

Air Hunger   71

At Long Last   72

STORYTELLING

The story of a life is
just a story,
and the self about which it tells
is gone to bone and filament
before we are through the telling.

And yet, it may not be wrong
to treasure these tales
of how we have come
to be what we are
in the fleet and flume.

The story of a life is just a story.
Expressive face, hands flourished
in the air, words flashing images
and one's true voice.
Who then is the storyteller?

I. GRACE

EMPTYING

The old woman's throat opens
after long holding in words, all the untold.
Something has been set in motion, a quickening
along the reluctant approach to death.
A bold curse issues. Accusation rises
in a dream of dark faces, voices
emanating from shadow.
To be special, unique in this world
—what we all harbor?
At worst to be spared the indignity of soiled diapers.
Returned to infantile.
But her shit is not sweet breast-fed,
her buttocks not smooth as peaches.
To our surprise, she is granted a long reprieve.
Night birds deny stench and sour stomach,
praise beauty. Still a chance
to clear out the cluttered closet, to embrace
the once-rejected. At last,
at ease before the arc of the unfolding.

GIVE AND TAKE

She meant it to be a giving thing—
time for her to leave
and leave a part of herself
—a final sorting.

The light-refracting crystal, polished silver,
pale hand-painted china—possessions
from another life, when she believed
in certainty.

She wanted each to take what was needed,
what was wanted, expecting that what
was chosen would have meaning
—hold a memory of her.

They came, bringing their mean spirits,
and took too much—
her gifts disappearing
without a word.

HALFWAY HOME

Get me out of here, she demands,
I do not belong here—
defiant in peach silk,
looking down
the hallway at the others.

Sent on an errand, I pass another,
abandoned in a wheelchair—
here to stay. She whispers,
Help me, I'm late for bingo
and have no shoes.

I, who can come and go,
offer no more
than a smile and touch.
For that, a stroked cheek,
You're pretty, I love you.

Returned to the misfit—
I paint her nails and assure,
You'll be home soon. She waves
good-bye, inspecting her fingers
to the bitter end.

THE MANICURE

The nail file, bowl of soapy water,
base and top coat,
coral polish on the table.

Holding her hand in mine,
shaping, stroking, I notice
my gentle teasing—how she benefits

from your passing. And I wonder, Mother,
if you are watching and if perhaps
her wrinkled and age-spotted hands

—almost as beautiful as yours were—
are yours,
if you feel me caring,

wishing for you. As if
somehow this can happen
simultaneously—even now.

COMBING MEMORY

Tenderness arising for this woman
who always thought she'd die
if she broke her hip. Her relieved sigh
as I run my fingers
through her once-red hair.

As my mother did long ago
through restless nights, toying
with curls clustered
all over my head.

What dreams she ushered—
called in from a carefree sky.
So sweet, little sister pulled taut
a stray, straight strand and cried,
My hair hurts.

Now here we are—
this second mother and I.
Her hip, her hair, everything
hurting.

Loopy from pain and Percocet—
adorable really. Perhaps
this, and not that
aloof grace she puts on,
is her truest nature.

I remember I once laid my head
in her lap, in need of comfort.
And as my mother's had,
her fingers became combs.

THE BLUE JAR

I bring the glass and pewter jar
she bought in Istanbul years ago
and once kept stocked with candies

and tear paper into strips
to record memories, thinking that
if she could savor, one last time,

the favors of her life,
she could then let them go—
the way a warm mouth melts all our sweets.

I expect her to speak
of her sons, the grandchildren, me—
but what comes instantly to her lips

is the memory of strolling down
Euclid Avenue in Cleveland,
arm in arm with Bud, the fresh gardenia

he bought from a street vendor each Sunday
pinned to her lapel. He had not been
the first man or the tallest to come through

the door of the dance hall, but the one,
from the moment she laid eyes on him,
she wanted.

After that she added simply,
my mother, Francis. With that,
the jar could hold no more.

FOR MY SAKE

Knowing her mind is prone to addle,
she asks the chaplain to preserve
her report of the sensations
she experienced in the night—

bladder and bowels emptying
just before the wrenched
tear of the very self
up and out of the body—

sensations so vivid that
when she opened her eyes
she implored of the nurse
standing beside her bed,

Am I in heaven?
She wants this written
on her pad of blue paper
so she can remember to tell me.

She knows I am listening—
as if grace can be learned
from the glimpses
she carries back.

A CHANGE IN THE WEATHER

Even as I wish for death
to come to her,

I find myself cursing
the too-early kill of green—
leaves that had no chance to change
and blaze against the autumn sky

deep blue. After a September snow,
they brown, then fall—all at once—
covering the ground in dry shrivel.

In youth a red-haired beauty, she has
lived more than a ninety-year turn. Now,
wasted and pale, she goes on and on,
sleeping the days away

in shrouded dream—her mind adrift,
her heart unfailing.

SHROUDED

Though she lay still under a white shroud,
she can see her body—like all the others
laid out in rows, face down.

The whole room is white, neither sterile
nor glaring. There is no glow—
just pale and cool as fresh snow.

No gates, no blinding light,
no voice or reassuring warmth.
This is her afterlife.

She wonders what the others are thinking
—if they too are thinking—
and if she is allowed to raise her head.
She has always followed the rules.

See her at nine, almost a century ago—
crossed ankles, starched blouse,
skirt pulled primly over her knees.

And later, her friend's father's hand
reaching over the back seat
and up between her legs.

Without ever being told,
she has known it is, almost always,
best not to tell.

She does not believe in hell
but is anxious to know
—if God or an angel would say—
what she must conform to next.

A CHANGE OF MIND

I thought she would die when
she broke her hip, like the old woman
I read about in the paper today, who fell,
startled by a small dog.

For more than a year, death is all
she has wanted.
How can it be then, with pain in her chest,
frightened, she changes her mind?

The ghost of my mother whispers,
Be kind, you can't understand yet.

Now what?
We review the group activities calendar.
She could listen to the *History of Scrabble,*
watch a travel video, play Bingo.

No, she'd rather stay in bed.
A romance novel, liverwurst in the room fridge,
a day without diarrhea
—she calls it *good.*

In bed, propped up by pillows and bolster,
so shrunken—
the common appearance of a body
feeding on itself to keep the core alive.

That man in the headlines weeks ago,
lost in the backcountry for sixteen hours,
trudging all night in deep snow. Saved,
though all ten toes and his heels blackened.

The core alive—where the heart resides
and so there must be that spark, soul-flame.

She teases a nurse, listens while
one talks about a raft trip,
nodding with sympathy when another
tells of her sick child.

The narrow bed holds
a lighted candle.

GETTING DOWN TO BASICS

I remember when she told me
she had lost control of her bowels,
and as she tried to get down on her knees
to clean up the mess,
she fell, sweeping

perfume and pill bottles off the counter,
and lay there
in feces and broken glass
until an aide answered the call bell.
I just want to die, she cried.
                    Oh God, as would I.

Yet today, bedridden, she describes
constipation, enemas and diaper changes
in a matter-of-fact way.
At the look on my face, she shrugs,
Dear, what can I do?

I suppose she is right—
whatever I think I cannot bear
                    is what will be asked of me.

SNOWBLIND

March storm blows down snow,
covering over
the dull and desolate

with its dazzling cold, making death
seem somehow lovely, even
desirable.

White field ripe with possibility,
the morning-after sky
paled with promise.

II. LAUGH OR CRY

AND WHAT OF HUMOR, KÜBLER-ROSS?

It seems not so very long ago,
she cowered under the covers,
dreading her heart's failure—
when no words could soothe her

nor our wish she could live
her last days fearless and forgiving.
Nor so long since, hip-shattered,
death was all she yearned for.

Now, resigned she will die
only in God's good time,
she sleeps the days away nibbling
at food once relished—

her once-large bearing frail.
Beauty remains in her hollowed face,
pale skin unfreckled by the sun,
stretched taut over bone.

Her mind as yet undimmed,
at our approach she lifts her head
from the pillow, winks and says,
I'm still here.

WORD CHOICE

Her hospice care has been
revoked.
What a word—
conjuring
wrongdoing and punishment.

Bedridden, sleeping
between food tray deliveries
and diaper changes—

all she has done is
stop
failing to thrive.

Temporarily suspended
would be more accurate.
For surely, at this point,
her license to live
is about to *expire.*

TAKING A GHOST FOR A DRIVE

The despondency has lifted
as if she had died and come back.

I come to take her for a drive along
the curving Peak to Peak to see
the aspen turned from green to gold.

But when the aide carries her
from the wheelchair into the car,
all I can think of is my own mother

and the patch of skin torn from her leg
when I, unskilled and impatient,
had done the same.

We say little, marveling at each backlit,
quaking tree that comes into view,
listening to a Streisand concert—

shedding a tear or two as the familiar lyrics,
like a whiff of scent,
evoke memories.

As we near the nursing home,
she says, *If I had died,*
I would not have had this day.

I love this woman and am glad
to do this for her. Still, I wish it were
my mother sitting beside me

and her hand I reach for. But
it was her death that taught me
the sweetness of such simple things.

FOUR BREATHS

I think of irises and how dramatically
they bloom. But the image shifts
to one of delicate petals, browned
and curled into an ugly fist.

In days of rain, I imagine bright sun
in a blue sky. But this fades
with the thought that soon it will be
as if it had never rained at all,
and I will curse the heat.

An image of lovers becomes the hope
that they will marry and,
if not, a wish
that their hearts stay soft, open.

I picture the bedridden one, cradling
a great-grandchild for the first time.
Even this won't hold—
what if she does not live
to see those indigo eyes?

A DEATHBED CONFESSION

No churchgoer, her father
was a big man with a booming voice.
Her mother, Catholic, slipped away

for Mass, scarf tied around her head,
but dared not take the children.
So she never went to church, spent

Sunday mornings dreaming
of marrying a rich man,
sober and kind—until

those weekend sleepovers and
church with her best friend's family.
She *loved going,* she says, her face

aglow. Was it the sermon, the stained glass,
the hymns? *No,* she says, turning coy.
Nothing like that. It was because

everyone there *fussed* over her—
thought her skin, her hair,
the ruffled dress and fake pearls

she'd packed so neatly,
so very
pretty.

NOT REALLY ABOUT THE HAIR

I find her,
bed-haired and wearing
an old hospital gown—

no longer caring
if her hair is styled, her nails painted,
her silk pajamas pressed.

But I care.

A small wish, in the midst
of open hands and parting waves,
that she could look

like herself—that familiar self,
irritating and fond.

And I find myself a child who,
momentarily distracted, lets go
a bright balloon

and begins to cry—
watching it hover and drift,
shrinking into infinite sky.

YOU'VE GOT TO BE KIDDING

The doctor wants to reduce the drugs
given to her for anxiety and depression
—moods that make
complete sense to me.

Consider—bedridden,
chin hairs sprouting, no bottom teeth,
drooped eyelid,
shitting in diapers.

Though she is aware of all this,
the drugs keep her placid,
and I wonder why he would
want to change them.

Oblivious to irony,
he explains his concern
about the *long-term* effect
on her 93-year-old liver.

A PLEA FOR A WITNESS

Long have I feared the many ways to lose
a mind along the aging road to death,
and so have found some comfort
in watching her mind observe her own

interminable approach. But I forgot the brain
is an organ and, like the heart and skin,
it too will fade, its function falter.
Her heart pumps slowly, her skin tears

as though protruded bones do the cutting
and, lately, her brain ceases to mind.
Buried scorns and hidden fantasies surface—
the landlord who knocked

on her door each day her husband
was away at sea, an Asian aide fondling
her shriveled breasts, the nurses starving her,
that strange expression on her face

as I gently brush crumbs from her chest.
She'd *die* if she knew what she was saying.
Deaf to this calamity of exposure,
only oblivion keeps her heart from breaking.

Mine breaks for her—and for me.
If the mind-cop goes off duty, how shattered
by meanness will my illusion be?
Beauty or Beast, Buddha or Bitch.

Urgently, I probe my liver where old
angers dungeon, feel them seeping down
to burn out in my right foot's tread.
At every dawn I sit on this pillow,

staying though my skull rattles.
What releases thought, I hope,
is not mattered-brain
and not even the idea of letting go—

but an *other* that hovers
above and near
like an enveloping mist.

DREAMING OF OBLIVION

The vase, brimming
with daylilies and the last

      of the lupine and purple campanula
      cut from our garden,

stands
on the table beside the bed
she cannot rise from.

               All there is for her now
               —enough.

Though the others keep,
the lilies bloom only

      for their day and, ever so
      silently, gently close

like lids folding over
to cover iris and black pupil—
and do not reopen.

THE DIE SPOT

~ a crossword puzzle clue

Drop of blood on the carpet,
yellow tape marks the spot
where the body was found?
No, three blank squares to fill.
Think of something other than death.
A laundry *vat* full of hot water,
the dye packet torn and emptied.
But that's cheating.
Dye is the wrong spelling. Face it.
A good place to die?
Alone in the middle of the night,
my mother rose from her bed—
to pee, sip water, call for help, who knows?
—and fell. Please God, instantly,
without fear, without wanting us near.
Still morning. In my breakfast bowl,
distraction. Blueberries, bananas,
watermelon—what Coco the chimp signed
sweet water. All those tiny black seeds. Oh,
the *die spot is a pip*—from one to six
black dots on a six-sided cube.
Gallows humor—laugh in the face of—
Gladys Knight and her backup singing,
I can see clearly now. But it's still raining.
Mind returns to its subject,
difficult as a Rubik's Cube. If dying
in a nursing home—no *Bleak House*—
well cared for, with a chance
to say a good good-bye, comes
at the price of a drawn-out death,
what would I choose? A matter of luck.
Blow on the dice in a cupped hand—
then roll.

III. TIMING

A BRIEF EXCHANGE

Her mind gaps. Once again, without intention,
she utters words that hurt him.

Gap filled, bridged, her eyelids redden—
without tears, this is how she cries.

She asks him to forgive her.
As he bends to kiss her forehead,

she takes his face in her frail hands
and says, *I want to kiss you.*

He thinks she holds on in fear of dying.
But her gesture seeks delay only

so she can leave him
in the world whole.

She does not realize this can happen
only when she is gone.

THE TIME IT TAKES

He no longer asks all
the whys and wherefores
　　　of the past they share—

standing by as his father berated him,
dressing him up as a little girl,
　　　boasting only of her other son.

He has ceased trying to get her
to remember what he remembers
　　　or believe what he believes.

She always claims not to know or to have
forgotten, and though she listens to
　　　his faith, it offers her no solace.

She is so frail, has lost so much
weight and color, he hardly recognizes
　　　his mother.

Finally, he can see her
for what she is now—a suffering,
　　　fearful, dying old woman.

For a long time, he sits, holding
her pale, bent-fingered hand.
　　　Then lays it down.

NOT A SUICIDE

Why am I still here?
she asks as I walk into the room.
This has gone on so long,
and I have said all I can say.
It is a gray place, this place
of not wanting to live
yet not yet dead.

She knows she can stop
eating, taking fluids
and she'd die
in a few days—
any pain or discomfort
ice-chipped and drugged away.

What stops her?

It's not that she believes
this would be a sin, or that
she must wait for God's taking.
And while there are much worse
ways to be dying, this undemented
enduring drags heavy.

Still, there is this—the impossibility
of certainty, the remote possibility
of hell, Dante's wild imaginings.
But most likely, it is simply
life's stiff-necked, heel-dug
obdurate
will.

DROUGHT'S END

Last night I woke
to a strange sound—

rain

falling through lead sky,
cold like bullets
firing wet.

This morning—life's insistence
in the stiff will of a new
blade of grass

with never a thought
of dry suicide.

RSVP

She wants to come to the wedding
—my son's, her grandson's—
knowing
death would be her escort.

I understand—I do, but
how dare she
risk ruining this day?

What if her heart finally fails,
what of her wish to die
peacefully in sleep?

I stay away for days
until I can speak
from a softened heart.

My hand strokes her shriveled arm
as I say, *You cannot come.*
You know it's impossible.

At my words, her face
looks like it would look
if she ever cried.

She turns her head,
averting her eyes. And I sit
in the silence of harder
than I thought this would be.

DEATH WISH

Walking by sumac and aspen
turning color in the fall,
with sun on their faces,
they look dull, already dead.

On my return, the sun
now at their backs,
they glow purple,
garnet and gold.

Please, when I am dying,
lying there in my bed
with no more need of books,
move the lamps behind me.

BOX OF DIVINITY

All it takes is time, patience
and a dry day.

Throughout a long life, she has been
given flowers, ribbon-tied
boxes of candy, and told
she is beautiful, sweet.

Heat sugar, corn syrup and water
to exactly the right temperature.

Aging, she has felt loved
when we do for her—
fix a lamp, give a manicure,
hang an old print on the wall.

Pour a slow, steady stream
into egg whites beaten to stiff peaks.

With less and less time left, time
matters more. So we sit by the bed,
calling up memories,
conjuring heaven.

Drop the divinity, light and airy,
with a twirl of the pushing spoon.

WE ARE ALL NEW

New skin in how many days?
The flaking and sluffing of cells—
cells of skin, hair, all the organs.

We are all dying,
parts of us aging or dying out
all the time.

They say there is no such thing
as time in eternity—that
past, present and future are one.

If this is so, and so it must be,
it cannot be
so great a difference to die.

SHE STILL SURPRISES ME

Today, face aglow, she asks if I'd seen
this morning's sunrise, calling it
the most beautiful she's ever seen.

A sign that she will die soon?
Or that, at last, she knows
there is no past, no future,

that this sunrise is unique in all of time
—no sunrise like it before or again—

and this display
—a fiery sun igniting clouds—
set against a window-square of sky,

moment by moment bluing,
is all there is.

DEAD AND I JUST DON'T KNOW IT

I call the doctor, the home,
leave frantic messages—
seeking explanation, resolution.
But no one answers, no one calls back.

The parking lot is empty, the interior dark.
The sign on the door says: *Open Sunday 10 a.m.*
It is 10:30. It must be morning—
the sun is out. But no one is here.

Surely this is just a bad dream
like the one from childhood
of my father dying.
But that was all too real.

As I walk away, I pass by
a window and expect
to see my reflection. But no—
there is only blank sky.

DO NO HARM

What misery.
All her muscles atrophying,
organs wearing out. Me, too.

Finally, hospice will take over again—
keep her comfortable, free of pain,
while not prolonging
this life she says she wants
no more part of.

The hospice nurse senses my relief,
whispering as we embrace,
Now you can let down. I suppose—

at least no more standing up
to those who would torment her
with pills and procedures,
good intentions and their well-meant
vacant hope.

IV. AMBIVALENCE

THE RIDE

The doctor says she will die soon.
He is new to caring for her.
We have heard this, thought this, before.

The chaplain says she saw her long-dead
mother in the doorway, beckoning
with a *Come with me* wave of her hand.

A sign perhaps?
Still, we know enough
not to begin to hope or grieve.

Do they think us heartless, think we lie
when we profess to love her? Have they never
felt nauseous on a roller coaster?

The same day, we get word her Medicaid file
has been closed. We hesitate to wrangle
on the chance this is no oversight but omen.

This morning the doctor finds her
sitting up, drinking coffee and eating
oatmeal with lots of brown sugar.
We say, *See Doc? Hold on.*

JUST A FEW MORE STEPS

She has been getting out of bed,
walking a long way without shoes.
But her bare feet are soft.
She denies flying. Everywhere

     looks just like this room,
her room. She does not believe
she belongs here,
worries about double rent.

       In her travels
she encounters no one expected—
not a dead husband, her mother,
a son at a young age.

Her breath comes shallow, rapid
through the panic. Dreams pervade.
Spirit keeps taking leave
of that worn body. When for a moment

     she returns—to herself—
she is reassured she has been here
all along, cared for by angels, wings
sewn to their shoulders.

       Her face falls,
and her bony fingers rake her hair—
she had been happy,
thinking she could walk again.

The spruce tree on the corner is invisible
from the bed. But each morning
a woman lies down
on the sheet of snow

beneath its low spread
of branch and needle,
remains there for hours
not moving.

She is lost.
Her shadow, one no sun can cast,
stitched to her left heel,
unraveling.

TOUCH IS THE LAST TO GO

I start to tell her the doctor thinks
she is much closer now. After all
she has said about wanting to die,
I assume this news will comfort her.

But those eyes, that barely stay open
these days, widen and stare. I swear
I can hear the questions
swirling in her head—*What's wrong?*
Maybe a blood test? Do I need surgery?

So I make light of what I'd begun to say
—*He's new, you'll fool him!*—
and quickly change the subject,
ask her about the past,
chat about my day.

She tires, shuts her eyes.
I brush her hair, stroke her forehead—
as if my fingers could discover
what she really wants.

ANTICIPATION

After the wondering comes to an end,
after the ups and downs, the stutter steps,
after the petal pulling—*will she, will she not?*—
after the burden of duty, the depressing
scene of skin and bones beneath a sheet,
after the effort of easing and cheering,
the bills and regulations, phone calls,
after the last four years succumb to forgetting—

after all this, maybe then,
memories of lighter times
will stir.

But for now, they lie numb, dull—
like a foot gone to sleep.

NOTHING TO DO BUT WAIT

Seen through the window, this gray
and cloud-filled sky betrays
no portent of delay, of finality. Unseen,
the North Star points true, but mostly
believing the sky will clear
brings little comfort. Up in thin air,
the time and shape of things
to come, vague and uncertain.
Will the old tree fall down,
will the child be born sweet and well,
will the old woman soon die
dreaming? Night is the worst.
Oh, no storm or blow,
no wail or hair-torn keening.
Just a tear muffled in a bunched pillow.
At dawn, an unhurried rain falls—
tap, tap, tap on leaf and pane,
constant, finger thrumming.
Nothing to do but busy these hands.
Baking is my friend Teresa's remedy.
Stir yeast and water, knead
dough in a big blue bowl. Seen
through the oven's glass door,
this loaf has the look of a waxing moon—
serenity rising.

WELCOME AND FAREWELL

Behind closed lids, the newborn dreams
of angels, of the swaddled, muffled realm
she came from the day before.

When her eyes open
—our glowing faces a blur—
a bond forms, strong as an uncut cord.

Back at the bedside, I cannot rouse
the old one though, stroking her arm,
I describe her great-grandchild.

A bubble of hope rises
unbidden, that our parting
may soon come.

Thus, when I return next day,
I confess my shoulders slump,
face falls. For at her name's call

—still clinging to the fragile thread
that binds her here—
she opens her eyes.

THE RIGHT QUESTION

A hook, a cane, half-moon, the winding way to a point.
In a whisper, a *hiss,* spoken by a poet.
What you don't want to hear, don't want to answer,

don't even have the answer for. Dismissed, still
it haunts, tugging at a coat sleeve.
Like the knob on a door to a hidden room,

the shovel at an ancient site,
the aloe that softens, crumbler of walls,
bower of flowers, of heads.

What removes blinders from the eyes
of a racehorse, what probes bone and heart,
what closes the circle.

So that, in the midst of battering wings,
shadow and relic—there at bottom,
you find treasure, the forgotten beforetime.

And now, like a red and blue parachute
ballooning at the ripcord pull, like the sea
that receives and raises up the cliff jumper,

like two strong arms that snatch you from the track
where you play *chicken* before a speeding train—
it is what saves you.

FATE OF TULIPS

Foolish flowers—
no memories stored underground
from this yearly rite of spring.
Undeterred,

they break the surface
bent on blooming,
only to be bowed and snow-frozen.
For a time,

refusing to notice them—
all too painful this early end
to colored determination and petaled will.
But that hurt too,

just another sort of loss,
closing my heart
like a muted, furled bud.
Now,

giving myself up to this,
they open—I open—
to warm spring sun.
We cannot help ourselves.

SUDDENLY AWARE OF HARDENING

In the blink of an eye,
—and all at once—
I soften, shield to loss
clattering to the floor.

And what was
—the jaded way of seeing—
is no more,
      as if it never were.

Like the vase that fades
into negative space when
—with a squint of a fresh eye—
once-unseen profiles emerge.

Once-solid ground shifting underfoot,
I rush to this second mother of mine,
all the way praying,
      Not yet, not yet.

Late summer's purple asters wilt by the bed.
Leaning in, face close to hers,
I, who days before had wished
her eyes not open,

call her back.
      Wake up, please wake up.
        She winks.

V. QUICKENED

TOO FAR GONE

We lay the infant on the coverlet
over her sunken chest,

bolsters on either side of the bed.
On the old one's face, deep pleasure

as if pulleyed up slowly—no spills—
hand over hand, from the bottom of a well.

This too—
ageless all-mothering etched

and surfacing in the grooves.
Yet *completely* passive. But not blank,

not empty. More like
an unrippled lake, a cloudless sky.

And an echo of a name or a word,
Hello! called down into that well.

As if even she thinks
this moment with this precious child

gives no purpose to her lingering,
no reason to prolong her misery.

UNDO THE PAST AND BE DONE

After a little talk, a little tenderness,
I am up and about, busy

organizing her closet,
dusting photos, watering
bamboo and peace lily—

       just as years ago
in my own mother's room
the day of the night she fell.

With a glance at the clock, I bend
to kiss her cheek, stroke her gray hair,
turn to grab my purse.

And for the first time ever,
she says, *I love you,* before I do.

Words, not heard in her childhood,
once so hard for her
to say at all.

       Words, like my mother's plea,
I just want to look at your face, words
I didn't know would mean *Good-bye.*

LAST WORDS

Shrunken body, withered skin
—some quality is departing,

but on its way, it speaks

in a voice we recognize
—yet deeper, unmuffled by form,
words that could not have been

uttered by someone fully in her flesh
—with such simplicity

it breaks the living open.

THE LURE OF CLAY

According to Sufi legend, God coaxed spirit into form
when He set the clay to dancing.

I want you in your body—

my eyes want to look at you,
my hands want to touch.

But what if
—just what if—

the surprise at death is this—

these bodies have been
what separate us,
keep us apart,

and rid of them
we are closer together
than ever—

as close as one. Still

it is so hard to let go,
to comprehend another way—

death's ravaging beauty.

AIR HUNGER

After the long lingering—suddenly
in transition.
No glow, no aura surrounds her,

no bright force enters the room.
No sitting up
in a flush and rush of last words. No.

Reality is this. Arms,
in a weak flailing, grasp
at something invisible in the air.

The weight of a sheet too heavy
on her heaving chest.
A purpling like bruises,

blood pooling at the elbows and feet.
The pain of a body as its organs
shut down one by one,

the panic of a body that cannot breathe.
Morphine for the pain,
Ativan for the panic.

Finally, this becomes the silent watch.
Mouth agape—
this dear old woman

a hooked fish flopped on a pier,
gills dying for a splash, a gulp—
one last sip.

AT LONG LAST

A tiny silver bird
    departs,
        long tail trailing
through the mist,
    no more
        encumbered by
the shape that clay assumes.

I too am lightened,
        the weight of waiting—
like a stone, lifted.
    No sting or prick,
        twinge or qualm.

Against a blue sky,
    embossed
clouds drift by.
    In bas-relief,
        death's enigmatic smile—
    a mercy.
One feather wafts down.

ACKNOWLEDGMENTS

The following poems have been previously published, in one form or another.

Aries: "A Change of Mind," "Shrouded"
Freefall: "Halfway Home"
Illya's Honey: "A Change in the Weather," "Just a Few More Steps"
Main Street Rag: "Getting Down to Basics"
Mountain Gazette: "Touch Is the Last to Go"
Mudfish: "Drought's End"
Pearl: "And What of Humor, Kübler-Ross?"
POEM, Huntsville Literary Association: "Dreaming of Oblivion"
Praxis: "The Lure of Clay"
Tiger's Eye: "Taking a Ghost for a Drive"
White Pelican: "The Blue Jar"
Words of Wisdom: "Snowblind"

In addition, "Emptying" won 2nd prize in the 2008 Writer's Studio Literary Contest (Arapahoe Community College, Denver, Colorado) and "A Plea for a Witness" was a finalist in the 2013 contest.

Thanks to family and friends for their support as we cared for and comforted my mother-in-law, Geraldine King, in her final years. Gratitude to the nurses and other staff at Manor Care of Boulder, who took excellent care of Gerri and became quite fond of her. I don't know what we would have done without Family Hospice of Boulder's emotional and spiritual counsel and support.

Once again, thank you to the Gamut poets—Ran Huntsberry, Karen Douglass, Carmella Santorelli, Jane Costain, Julie Ascarrunz, and Judy Satterlee—without whom these poems would not be as strong and who, week after week, read them as they came up and through in my journey alongside Gerri.

Cover design by Bryce King; interior book design by Diane Kistner; PT Serif text with Century Gothic titling

About FutureCycle Press

FutureCycle Press is dedicated to publishing lasting English-language poetry books, chapbooks, and anthologies in both print-on-demand and ebook formats. Founded in 2007 by long-time independent editor/publishers and partners Diane Kistner and Robert S. King, the press incorporated as a nonprofit in 2012. A number of our editors are distinguished poets and writers in their own right, and we have been actively involved in the small press movement going back to the early seventies.

The FutureCycle Poetry Book Prize and honorarium is awarded annually for the best full-length volume of poetry we publish in a calendar year. Introduced in 2013, our Good Works projects are anthologies devoted to issues of universal significance, with all proceeds donated to a related worthy cause. Our Selected Poems series highlights contemporary poets with a substantial body of work to their credit; with this series we strive to resurrect work that has had limited distribution and is now out of print.

We are dedicated to giving all of the authors we publish the care their work deserves, making our catalog of titles the most diverse and distinguished it can be, and paying forward any earnings to fund more great books.

We've learned a few things about independent publishing over the years. We've also evolved a unique, resilient publishing model that allows us to focus mainly on vetting and preserving for posterity the most books of exceptional quality without becoming overwhelmed with bookkeeping and mailing, fundraising activities, or taxing editorial and production "bubbles." To find out more about what we are doing, come see us at www.futurecycle.org.

The FutureCycle Poetry Book Prize

All full-length volumes of poetry published by FutureCycle Press in a given calendar year are considered for the annual FutureCycle Poetry Book Prize. This allows us to consider each submission on its own merits, outside of the context of a contest. Too, the judges see the finished book, which will have benefitted from the beautiful book design and strong editorial gloss we are famous for.

The book ranked the best in judging is announced as the prize-winner in the subsequent year. There is no fixed monetary award; instead, the winning poet receives an honorarium of 20% of the total net royalties from all poetry books and chapbooks the press sold online in the year the winning book was published. The winner is also accorded the honor of being on the panel of judges for the next year's competition; all judges receive copies of all contending books to keep for their personal library.

www.ingramcontent.com/pod-product-compliance
Lightning Source LLC
Chambersburg PA
CBHW070011100426
42741CB00012B/3192